PORTUGAL AND THE WAR OF THE SPANISH SUCCESSION

T0364217

PORTUGAL & THE WAR
OF THE
SPANISH SUCCESSION

A Bibliography
with some Diplomatic Documents

by

EDGAR PRESTAGE
M.A., D.Litt.

Late Camoens Professor in the University
of London, King's College

CAMBRIDGE
At the University Press
1938

CAMBRIDGE
UNIVERSITY PRESS

University Printing House, Cambridge CB2 8BS, United Kingdom

Cambridge University Press is part of the University of Cambridge.

It furthers the University's mission by disseminating knowledge in the pursuit of education, learning and research at the highest international levels of excellence.

www.cambridge.org
Information on this title: www.cambridge.org/9781107585850

© Cambridge University Press 1938

First published 1938
First paperback edition 2015

A catalogue record for this publication is available from the British Library

ISBN 978-1-107-58585-0 Paperback

CONTENTS

Preface   *page* vii

Bibliography   I

Appendices:

    I. Extracts from the *Instrucções ineditas a Marco Antonio de Azevedo Coutinho*, by D. Luis da Cunha   13

    II. The close of volume IV of the *Memorias* of the same   17

    III. Instruction of 18th June 1709 to the Conde de Tarouca   19

    IV. Instruction of 30th June 1709 to the same   29

    V. Instruction of 6th August 1709 to the same   32

    VI. Questions of D. Luis da Cunha   36

PREFACE

Except for chapters in general Histories, which are inadequate, we possess no printed description of the political, military, and diplomatic aims and action of Portugal during the period from the death of Charles II of Spain to the Peace Treaties of 1713 and 1715 with France and Spain. The published monographs, even in Portuguese, are not very many, but the manuscript material in various languages is abundant, as will appear in the following pages. When consulting the diplomatic papers it will be well to remember the names and dates of the Portuguese representatives in foreign Courts. These were: in France from 1699 to 1704 José da Cunha Brochado; in England from 1696 to 1712 D. Luis da Cunha and also from 1710 to 1715 Cunha Brochado; in Holland from 1694 to 1709 Francisco de Sousa Pacheco and from 1710 to 1716 the Conde de Tarouca, who was appointed Extraordinary Ambassador and first Plenipotentiary to the Congress of Utrecht with D. Luis da Cunha as his colleague.

The Portuguese Secretaries of State were: from 1688 to 1702 Mendo de Foios Pereira, from 1702 to 1703 José de Faria, from 1703 to 1705 D. Antonio Pereira da Silva, from 1705 to 1707 D. Thomás de Almeida and from 1707 to 1736 Diogo de Mendonça Corte Real.[1]

A useful introduction to the subject is provided by *An Account of the Court of Portugal under the Reign of the present King Dom Pedro II* (London, 1700; French version Paris, 1702); it was published anonymously but written by the Revd John Colbatch, Chaplain of the British Factory in Lisbon, during seven years at the end of the seventeenth century. He was an intelligent observer and consulted reliable authorities. His book contains detailed information on Portuguese history for the half century preceding the War of the Spanish Succession, and elaborate descriptions

[1] Luis Teixeira de Sampayo, *O Arquivo Historico do Ministerio dos Negocios Estrangeiros*, pp. 99–102, 114. Coimbra, 1925.

⟨ vii ⟩

of the character and attainments of King Pedro and his ministers, with chapters on the relations of Portugal with the Holy See, France, Spain and England. These need to be checked from the more complete and documented sources published in modern times. Reference may also be made to the *Mémoires* attributed to Théophile Daupinéaut, though his judgments on public men are often rendered suspect by his sarcastic disposition.[1]

Translations of passages from the works of D. Luis da Cunha and of some diplomatic documents will be found in the Appendices. He is perhaps the most famous of Portuguese diplomats and spent most of his life in foreign Courts in the service of Pedro II and John V, who succeeded his father in 1706. In the science of diplomacy D. Luis was a "fifth Gospel" to many of his countrymen and he came to be regarded as an oracle in Paris where he died in 1740 at the age of seventy-eight.

I should add that my Bibliography is only tentative and not meant to be exhaustive. Sr. Gastão de Melo e Matos has been good enough to assist in its compilation with his wide and detailed knowledge of the subject.

E. P.

10 *October*, 1938

---

[1] Published in part by me under the title *Memorias sobre Portugal no reinado de D. Pedro II* in *Arquivo Historico de Portugal*, vol. ii. Lisbon, 1936.

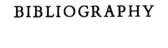

BIBLIOGRAPHY

BIBLIOGRAPHY

A. TREATIES AND OTHER COLLECTIONS OF PRINTED DOCUMENTS

Actes, Mémoires et autres pièces authentiques concernant la paix d'Utrecht. 6 vols. Utrecht, 1714–15.

BORGES DE CASTRO, J. F., and BIKER, J. F. J. *Collecção de Tratados,* etc. Vols. I, II, IX and X. Lisbon, 1856, 1872 and 1873.

MIGNET, F. A. M. *Négociations relatives à la succession d'Espagne sous Louis XIV. Collection de documents inédits.* 4 vols. Paris, 1835–42.

Recueil des Instructions données aux Ambassadeurs et Ministres de France. Portugal. Ed. by the Vicomte de Caix de Saint Aymour. Paris, 1886.

SANTAREM, VISCONDE DE, and others. *Quadro Elementar,* etc. Vols. IV, pt 2 and V. Paris, 1844–5; and vol. XVIII. Lisbon, 1880.

VAST, HENRI. *Les Grands Traités du règne de Louis XIV.* Vol. III. Paris, 1899.

B. CONTEMPORARY PRINTED NARRATIVES

BERWICK, DUKE OF. *Mémoires.* Coll. Petitot, vols. LXV and LXVI. Paris, 1828.

BOLINGBROKE, VISCOUNT. *The Study and Use of History, Letters* vi–viii. With an introduction by G. M. Trevelyan. Cambridge, 1932. A defence of the Treaty of Utrecht.

—— *Letters and Correspondence.* 4 vols. London, 1798.

COUTO CASTELO BRANCO, ANTONIO DO. *Comentarios sobre as Campanhas de 1706 e 1707 em Espanha.* Ed. by G. de Melo e Matos. Coimbra, 1931.

—— *Memorias e Observações Militares,* etc. Vol. III. Lisbon, 1740.

COXE, WILLIAM. *Memoirs of the Duke of Marlborough.* Ed. by J. Wade. Vols. II and III. London, 1893.

CUNHA, D. LUIS DA. *Instrucções ineditas a Marco Antonio de Azevedo Coutinho.* Ed. by Pedro de Azevedo and Antonio Baião. Coimbra, 1930.

Du-Guay Trouin, M. de. *Vie écrite de sa main.* Ed. by H. Malo. Paris, 1922.

Galway, Earl of. *Cartas ao 2do Conde de Assumar.* Ed. by G. de Melo e Matos, Lisbon, 1931, and published by the review *Historia.* The letters are dated from 1706 to 1711. Assumar was Portuguese Ambassador to the Archduke Charles, claimant to the crown of Spain.

Louis XIV. *Correspondance avec M. Amelot son Ambassadeur en Espagne 1705–9.* 2 vols. Nantes, 1864.

Louville, Marquis de. *Mémoires.* 2 vols. Paris, 1818.

Marlborough's Dispatches. Ed. by Sir George Murray. 5 vols. London, 1845.

Soares da Silva, José. *Gazeta em forma de carta* (1701–1716). Vol. I. Lisbon, 1933.

Swift, Jonathan. *The Conduct of the Allies.* Oxford, 1916.

Tarouca, Conde de. *Cartas dirigidas ao Cardeal da Cunha.* Ed. by A. de Gusmão Navarro. 1927. The letters are dated 1712–14 and are from the Hague and Utrecht.

Tessé, Maréchal de. *Mémoires.* 2 vols. Paris, 1806.

Torcy, Marquis de. *Mémoires, 1687–1713.* Coll. Michaud et Poujoulet, Nouv. Coll. III, 8. Paris, 1850.

—— *Journal, 1709–11.* Ed. by J. Masson. Paris, 1903.

Ursins, Princesse des, et Mme de Maintenon. *Lettres inédites.* 4 vols. Paris, 1826.

An Account of the Earl of Peterborow's Conduct in Spain. London, 1707.

An Account of the Earl of Galway's Conduct in Spain and Portugal. London, 1711. A reasoned defence of Galway containing an account of the operations of the Portuguese armies and English and Dutch auxiliaries from 1704 to 1709.

Remarks upon the Account lately published of the Earl of Galway's conduct in Spain and Portugal in a letter to a friend in Holland. London, n.d. The title of this pamphlet, which does not appear to be in the British Museum, was kindly supplied by Sr. Melo e Matos.

A Detection of the Earl of Galway's Conduct at Almanza in the following original Letters, etc. London, 1711. There are four letters, written respectively by

Schonenberg, Dutch Ambassador at Lisbon, the Count de Noyelles, Dutch General in Spain, Brigadier Drinborn, who was in the battle, and the Count de Cordona. Galway is blamed for having fought the battle, that is, for having persuaded das Minas to do so.[1]
Impartial Enquiry into the Management of the War in Spain. London, 1712. A defence of Galway against Peterborough.

Relaçam da Campanha de Alemtejo no Outono de 1712, com o Diario do sitio e gloriosa defensa da Praça de Campo Mayor, Recopilada das Memorias dos Generaes. Lisbon, 1714. A detailed and valuable account of the campaign of 1712 and the gallant defence of Campo Mayor against the Marques de Bay in forty-seven closely printed pages.

C. LATER PRINTED NARRATIVES

ALBRECHT, JOHANNES. "Englands Bemühungen um den Eintritt Portugals in die Grosse Allianz (1700–1703)" in *Abhand. Bremer Wissenschaftlichen Gesellschaft,* 1933. A detailed account based on English, Portuguese and Dutch MS sources.

ALMEIDA, FORTUNATO DE. *Historia de Portugal.* Vol. IV. Coimbra, 1926.

BAUDRILLART, A. *Philippe V et la Cour de France.* Paris, 1890.

BEM, D. THOMAS CAETANO DO. *Memorias historicas chronologicas dos Clerigos Regulares.* 2 vols. Lisbon, 1792–4. Vol. II (pp. 34–162) contains a minute account from the *Memorias* of D. Luiz Caetano de Lima (chaplain and secretary of the Conde de Tarouca) of the latter's negotiations in London and at the Congress of Utrecht down to the Peace Treaty between Portugal and Spain.

BRAZÃO, DR. EDUARDO. *Portugal no Congresso de Utrecht* 1712–1715. Lisbon, 1933.

—— *O Conde de Tarouca em Londres* 1709–1710. Lisbon, 1936.

CONCEIÇÃO, FREI CLAUDIO DA. *Gabinete Historico.* 17 vols. Lisbon, 1818–31. Vols. V to XI deal with the reigns of Pedro II and John V.

[1] In 1706, when Galway wished to return to England, Sunderland wrote to Earl Rivers to say that it was necessary he should stay on, "considering the influence he has on the Portuguese and that nobody has been able to manage them but him". Public Record Office, Miscellaneous Foreign Entry Books, vol. 208, p. 17. Referring to Almanza, Galway declared: "I had not the command of that army...but the Marquis das Minas from whom I always received orders." N. Tindal, *The History of England,* by Rapin, vol. IV, book xxvi, p. 7.

Courcy, Marquis de. *La Coalition de 1701 contre la France*. 2 vols. Paris, 1886.

Hill, D. J. *History of European Diplomacy*. Vol. iii. London, 1914.

Horn, D. B. *British Diplomatic Representatives, 1698–1789*. Camden Society, vol. xlvi. London, 1932.

Legrelle, A. *La Diplomatie française et la Succession d'Espagne*. 4 vols. Paris, 1888–92.

Lodge, Sir R. "The Spanish Succession" in *History*, vol. xii, no. 48. January, 1928.

—— "The Treaties of 1703" in *Chapters in Anglo-Portuguese Relations*. Ed. by E. Prestage. Watford, 1935.

Melo e Matos, G. de. *O ultimo Almirante de Castela em Portugal* (1702–1705). Lisbon, 1937. Offprint from vol. ii of the *Trabalhos da Associação dos Arqueologos*.

—— *Espiões e Agentes Secretos nos principios do seculo XVIII*. Published by *Miscelanea*, Oeiras, 1931.

Parnell, Colonel Arthur. *The War of Succession in Spain*. London, 1905. The best monograph in English, and the MS sources explored for the first time are numerous. The narrative is, however, unfair to the Portuguese, for though they supplied much larger forces than their allies, very little is said about them. The author repeats English complaints of their actions or inaction, but omits their reasons and counter-charges.

Peres, Professor Damião. *A diplomacia portuguesa e a Successão de Espanha, 1700–1704*. Barcellos, 1931. A valuable little book, based on Portuguese authorities, printed and unprinted.

—— and others. *Historia de Portugal*. Vol. vi, chap. 8. Barcellos, 1934.

Quincy, Marquis de. *Histoire militaire du règne de Louis le Grand*. 7 vols. 1726. D. Luis da Cunha considered that Berwick's victory at Almanza was due to the flight of a large part of the Portuguese cavalry (*Instrucções ineditas a Marco Antonio de Azevedo Coutinho*, p. 91) and this has generally been the English view, but Quincy in his description of the battle from the French side (vol. v, pp. 399–408) does not support it, nor does Berwick himself in his *Memoirs*. A full account of du-Guay Trouin's successful attack on Rio de Janeiro will be found in vol. vi (pp. 603–30), together with a fine engraving of the bay, city and forts, showing the disposition of the French fleet.

⟨ 6 ⟩

RONCIÈRE, CHARLES DE LA. *Histoire de la marine française*. Vol. VI. Paris, 1932.

SOUSA, D. ANTONIO CAETANO DE. *Historia da Casa Real Portuguesa*. 12 vols. Lisbon, 1735–48. See vols. VII, VIII, XI and XII, pt 2. The last volume has a biography of the Marques das Minas, commander-in-chief of the Portuguese army and English and Dutch contingents which occupied Madrid in 1706 and, reinforced by some Germans and Huguenots, lost the battle of Almanza in 1707.

STANHOPE, EARL. *History of the War of Succession in Spain*. London, 1832.

—— *Spain under Charles II*. London, 1844.

TREVELYAN, PROF. G. M. *England under Queen Anne*. Blenheim. Pp. 259, 298, 300–3. London, 1930.

WILLIAMS, A. F. B. *Stanhope*. Oxford, 1932.

D. CONTEMPORARY MANUSCRIPT MATERIAL

(1) London. Public Record Office. State Papers Foreign. Portugal, bundles 16 to 23. Foreign Entry Books, vols. 108 to 113. Foreign Ministers (in England), bundles 37, 38. Miscellaneous Foreign Entry Books, vols. 195–7, 207, 208, 210, 211.

State Papers Foreign. Spain, bundles 75 to 84 cover the years 1692 to 1715.

British Museum. Add. MSS 29,590–1 (Finch Hatton papers, letters of John and Paul Methuen); Add. MS 21,491 (letters of Paul Methuen); Add. MS 34,335 (Southwell papers, letters of Paul Methuen and William Blathwayt[1]); Add MS 38,159 (letters of John Methuen to Ormonde); Add. MSS 28,056–7 (letters of John and Paul Methuen, Galway and Peterborough to Godolphin); Egerton MS 891 (letters of Lord Galway, 1706–7); Stowe MSS 467 (diary of Colonel J. Richards, 1704–5) and 468 (letterbook of same).

Add. MSS 20,817–18. *Memorias da Paz de Utrecht*, by D. Luis da Cunha, 2 vols. The narrative begins with the Peace of the Pyrenees and reaches to the opening of the Congress; these illuminated volumes were presented by the author to John V and his Queen and contain fine engravings. There is an inferior copy in Add. MSS 15,587 and 15,178–9.

---

[1] William Blathwayt was the Acting Secretary of State who attended King William III during his absences on the Continent and on these occasions English Envoys in Foreign Courts were ordered to correspond with and take orders from him as the King's mouthpiece. William III was his own permanent Foreign Secretary.

Three later volumes are to be found in Portuguese libraries: vols. III and IV in the Biblioteca Nacional, Lisbon, Pombalina 449 and 450, and vol. V in the Library of the Academia das Ciências, 595 azul. This last volume relates the secret negotiations of the English Tory Government with France.

There seems to be no copy in London of another but unfinished work of da Cunha, *Tradução e Paraphrasi dos Tratados de Utrecht*.

Edited by Sr. Melo e Matos, the *Memorias* are being published by the review *Historia*, and the many copies of the work and of the *Tradução e Paraphrasi*, with their respective locations, are described in his introduction. These two works were not meant for publication, each volume was offered by the author to a different personage, and complete sets are hard to find together.

Add. MS 20,819. *Cartas sobre as negociações de Inglaterra escritas pelo Inviado Joseph da Cunha Brochado aos nossos Plenipotenciarios em Utrecht.* 1710–15. The value of this collection is considerably reduced by the effect of a note at the beginning: "These letters, as appears from their contents, were written about the affairs treated at Utrecht which depended on the Court of England....All the letters I wrote were not copied here, because a large number of them contained some circumstances which I considered ought to be suppressed, on the ground that they needed perfect notes to make them intelligible and, without these, they might be interpreted in such a way as to disfigure the truth."

Add. MS 15,182 contains Cunha Brochado's letters for the same period addressed to the Conde de Vianna, Master of the Palace. Add. MS 22,210 has correspondence between the Earl of Strafford and the Conde de Tarouca, 1712–14.

(2) Paris. Archives of the Ministry of Foreign Affairs. *Correspondance de Portugal.* Vols. XXXI and XXXIV to XLIX.

(3) Lisbon. *Relações de D. Luis da Cunha pendente a sua Residencia na Corte de Londres.* These entry books of da Cunha's official letters from London are mostly in the Torre do Tombo, but one or more volumes have found their way to the Ajuda Library. They begin in 1697. The same Archives possess the entry books of his correspondence and that of the Conde de Tarouca with Diogo de Mendonça relating to the negotiations at the Congress of Utrecht and also the entry books (Registos) of the correspondence of Sousa Pacheco with the Court of Lisbon from Holland.

The *Memorias* of D. Luiz Caetano de Lima in seven volumes regarding the negotiations of the Conde de Tarouca in England and Holland are at the Biblioteca Nacional. Their contents are set out by Sr. Melo e Matos in his study,

Noticia de alguns Memorialistas Portugueses, Lisbon, 1930, an offprint from the review *Nação Portuguesa*, 6th series, nos. 4–6. One or more of the volumes were evidently used by D. Thomas Caetano do Bem in his printed work already mentioned.

The Biblioteca de Ajuda has a number of diplomatic MSS and among them six volumes of the entry books and private correspondence of Cunha Brochado from Paris, London and Utrecht and his negotiations; cods. 49/x/36–41.

Turning from diplomatic to military history, the Torre do Tombo possesses an extensive collection of documents belonging to the Conselho de Guerra, while there is an entry book of the Duque de Cadaval (vol. ix) germane to our subject at the Biblioteca Nacional, cod. 749, Fundo Geral. In this library will also be found four volumes of letters addressed to the Conde de Assumar by various correspondents during the war; cods. 8542, 8545–6 and 8551, Fundo Geral.

No. 8542 contains the *Cartas de Galway* previously mentioned and also letters of Paul Methuen, Earl Stanhope, Lord Lexington, John, Duke of Argyll, Thomas Leffever and thirty-six of Peterborough. Most of these letters are originals and they belong to the years 1705 to 1713. No. 8545 has letters of Earl Stanhope and the Duque de Uzeda; No. 8546 has letters of D. Manuel Caetano de Sousa and No. 8551 has letters of the Marques de Fontes.

The *Diario Belico* of Frei Domingos da Conceição in the Library of the Academia das Ciências gives a minute account of the campaigns of the Portuguese army in Spain from 1706 to 1712.

Tarouca Archives. These rich family archives[1] contain: *Cartas de Diogo de Mendonça para o Conde de Tarouca*, 1709–33 and the following series of letters of the Conde de Tarouca: *Collecção de Cartas para Diogo de Mendonça*. 3 vols. 1709–14; *Collecção de Cartas para os Marquezes de Alegrete*. 22 vols. 1709–14; *Copia de tres Cartas ao Marquez de Alegrete sobre o Tratado de Utrecht*. 1715.

(4) Evora. Biblioteca Publica. *Cartas originaes do Conde de Tarouca ao Conde de Assumar*, 1709–1712.

---

[1] Vide *Catalogo dos Manuscriptos da Antiga Livraria dos Marquezes de Alegrete, dos Condes de Tarouca e dos Marquezes de Penalva*, pp. 43–7. Lisbon, 1898. The Marques de Alegrete was not only brother of Tarouca, but First Minister in fact, though not in name. He was the chief adviser of Pedro II in foreign policy, but in domestic affairs the Duque de Cadaval enjoyed greater influence. By his relationship with the Royal House, great possessions and appointments, the latter was the first subject in the realm. He fell out of favour on the accession of John V.

Memorias pertencentes á historia da paz de Utrecht, by D. Luiz Caetano de Lima. 4 vols. They consist mainly of documents relating to the Congress dated from 1711 to 1715.[1]

(5) The Spanish authorities on the subject, printed and unprinted, are catalogued by B. Sánchez Alonso in *Fuentes de la Historia Española e Hispano-Americana,* 2nd ed., vol. I, pp. 571–94. Madrid, 1927.

[1] *Catalogo dos Manuscriptos da Biblioteca Publica Eborense,* vol. III, pp. 388, 396–416. Lisbon, 1870. The Minutes of the Portuguese Council of State would have been valuable for the diplomatic history of the period, but their whereabouts is unknown. It was formerly supposed that they had been destroyed, together with the building that housed them, in the great Lisbon earthquake of 1755, but doubts have recently been cast upon this belief on the ground that the Council's Minutes of later date are also missing.

APPENDICES

I
EXTRACTS FROM THE *INSTRUCÇÕES INEDITAS A MARCO ANTONIO DE AZEVEDO COUTINHO*, BY D. LUIS DA CUNHA (COIMBRA, 1930)

p. 17. The Portuguese Ministers were the only ones at the Congress of Utrecht who were not given any means[1] to be well informed, or to corrupt the English, who had the role of mediators, and it was late when an attempt was made to remedy this mistake, for the Duke of Ossuna, on opening his purse, had Lord Strafford at once in his pocket.[2]

p. 33. William III of England, desiring to persuade me that Pedro II ought to leave the Alliance into which he had entered with Spain and France[3] and join the one he had just concluded with the Emperor and Dutch Republic, spoke these words to me, that if all the Powers of Europe were to see it with their own eyes, they would find that the time had come to abate the insupportable pride and insatiable ambition of Louis XIV, because he had taken upon him the defence of Spain, which was so heavy a load that he would fall under it and he had a good experience of this because he had borne it on his shoulders for so many years, and in truth that great Prince was not mistaken, for you and I have seen the extremity to which the said Monarch was reduced to keep that crown for his grandson.

p. 39. D. Pedro II, seeing at the end of the last century that Louis XIV accepted the will which Charles II had made in favour of his grandson, the Duke d'Anjou, contrary to the Partition Treaty which the said King had guaranteed and that in this way he would have a Bourbon Prince as neighbour, considered that for his security, as he no longer possessed what it gave him when a Prince of the House of Austria ruled in Spain, it was necessary to make an alliance with Philip V and his grandfather[3] from which he

[1] Money.
[2] The association of Strafford with Ossuna to the prejudice of Portugal is mentioned by Cunha Brochado more than once. Add. MS 20,819, British Museum, fols. 161, 165.
[3] By the Treaties of 18th June 1701.

would derive some advantage. He did so with the result that Philip V ceded him the ownership of the Colony of Sacramento, which would certainly have been a good thing if the condition had not been added that he was to enjoy it as he had it at the then present time, which came to be as was stipulated in the Provisional treaty.[1] This condition gave us much trouble at the Congress of Utrecht and I always wondered how our Ministers could have agreed to that clause which made the cession useless, especially at a time when the two Crowns had absolute need of an alliance with us and would not have failed to delete it, if we had insisted. But as the object of D. Pedro was not only to safeguard his dominions but to add to their extent, which would contribute to the same end, he listened to the proposals of the Maritime Powers and broke the Treaty he had just made with the two Crowns to ally with their foes[2] in consideration of the increase of boundaries they promised him, that is in Estremadura the fortresses of Badajoz, Albuquerque, Valencia and Alcantara and in Galicia la Guardia, Tuy, Bayona and Vigo with their dependencies. In America the Rivers Plate and Vicente Pinzón[3] were to divide the territories of the two Crowns[4] both on the South and North.

I will not enter into the question as to whether the good faith which ought to direct the act of rulers allowed this clear infraction, although the temptation was great both to enlarge our boundaries and to secure them on the Continent and outside it, seeing that the colours with which it was sought to be excused in an ill-drawn Manifesto[5] left it more shady, especially as there was no evident or immediate danger in observing the Treaty, and this is almost the same as my reply when the King asked me if in conscience and honour he could abandon the alliance he had made with France and Castile. For I took the liberty of telling him that he had made an interior and natural alliance with the obligation of maintaining his subjects in peace and security, so that as the contract with the two Crowns was later in date and a civil one, there was no doubt that whenever His

---

[1] Of 7th May 1681. Borges de Castro, *op. cit.* vol. IX, p. 342.
[2] By the Treaty of 16th May 1703.
[3] Or Oyapoc.   [4] I.e. Portugal and Spain.
[5] Printed by Borges de Castro, *op. cit.* vol. II, p. 198.

Majesty thought he could not sustain the first without violating the second, it followed that he could and ought for greater reasons to break his word, under the circumstances referred to by authors who have treated this delicate matter. But as His Majesty's question did not comprise the second part, that is a confederation with the enemies of those who were formerly his allies to make war on them, I was not called upon to go farther and I should have found myself much embarrassed, if I had been obliged to do so.

But it is remarkable that as soon as we had made this treaty, although the Archduke was a long way from conquering Spain, the Emperor sent M. Zinzerling to London to elude the cession of Badajoz on the pretext that Castilian Estremadura would be left open without this fortress. I at once advised our Court of this, so that it might take its measures accordingly, nevertheless I will add that we did not know how to use this good opportunity in regard to the Maritime Powers,[1] who left the Emperor and Archduke to make sacrifices by the cession of the fortresses on our frontiers after they had been captured and yet gave nothing of their own, except certain subsidies and assistances which were indispensable, when we ought to have asked them for the revocation of the infamous and ruinous commercial treaties we had made with them, substituting others more fair and less burdensome, to which they would have been compelled to agree to secure their aims, after having undertaken to make war on the two Crowns, because without the Portuguese harbours they had no means to introduce the Archduke into Spain or to shelter the fleets which they were to send to the Mediterranean.[2] This can easily be proved for I remember that Lord Nottingham, then Secretary of State, said, when we were about to sign this league, that he risked his head if he agreed to Articles 7 and 8, because the honour of the English flag would be prostituted by the preference given to that of Portugal when the allied fleets came together. On this account Queen Anne was obliged to summon the Great Council to Hampton Court and there Lord Godolphin, Lord High Treasurer of

[1] The printed text has *provincias* for *potencias*, a manifest error.
[2] "We are in such absolute necessity of having their port [Lisbon] that nothing must be omitted that can reasonably be done towards keeping them in the alliance." Sunderland to Methuen, Miscellaneous Foreign Entry Books, vol. 208, p. 175.

England and Prime Minister, seeing the importance of the affair (for before entering the Council I told him that I had orders to break off the Treaty, if these articles were not admitted), adopted the excuse of informing his fellow ministers that the occasion would never arise, because the number of Portuguese ships would never exceed that of the English when they were joined for some operation, which was the case of the preference and this sufficed for the Treaty to be ratified without alteration. Such was the need and opinion the English had of our alliance, for recalling our victories over the Castilians,[1] they imagined that with us on their side they would win the war. I confess I thought then that Pedro II had repented of having entered into the negotiation because our Ministers could not have thought that the English, who are so jealous of the honour of their flag, would yield it to the Portuguese, and that in this way with the refusal of England they desired to destroy the new alliance so that we might get out of what we had arranged, or at least remain neutral. So much so that the first instructions which John Methuen brought to Portugal were to propose neutrality to us and he asked me to indicate a person in Lisbon who could draw up a paper to which our Ministers would give attention and as I was on good terms with Manuel Gomes de Palma I suggested him, knowing that the paper would be well drafted and well paid for, as actually happened; but Gomes de Palma advised Methuen to begin his negotiation by persuading us to an alliance, like that which the Maritime Powers had made with the Emperor, for if we did not listen to it, he would always be able to propose neutrality. Methuen took his advice and seeing that he was listened to, returned to England where he was accused, chiefly by Lord Nottingham, of not having carried out his instructions, which only referred to our neutrality, but Lord Godolphin and the other ministers decided that he should return to Lisbon to carry on the new negotiation which went to the root of the matter, because ours was the only treaty in which it was agreed to take the Crown of Spain from Philip and put it on the head of the Archduke Charles, for it followed that we could not afford to have as a neighbour one whom we had just offended so gravely in his honour and profit.

[1] I.e. the Spaniards in the twenty-eight years' war from 1640 to 1668.

II

THE CLOSE OF VOLUME IV OF THE *MEMORIAS* OF D. LUIS DA CUNHA. (COD. 450 POMBALINA, BIBLIOTECA NACIONAL, LISBON)

Thus ended with the Peace of Portugal[1] the famous Congress of Utrecht, which for us lasted from January 1712 until April 1715. We did not obtain in this Peace Treaty the advantages we sought in that of Alliance,[2] which were an extension of territory which would also serve as a barrier; but the reader of these *Memoirs* will see that since our Court by its orders of 2nd April, 3rd June, 3rd and 15th July, 12th, 13th, 23rd August and others instructed us to follow that of England, which had sacrificed us before the Congress opened, it was impossible to obtain what we sought under this head. However, he will observe that though we were instructed by the dispatches of 8th April 1713 to conclude the peace without any other advantages than peace itself, and by the dispatches of August 5th we were told to abandon the claim to all sums owing in respect of the Asiento[3] by way of compensation for the Buenos Ayres ships,[4] and even to pay the English and Dutch the cargo which came in them and finally to content ourselves with the restitution of the Colony of Sacramento in the form stipulated in the Treaty of 1701, nevertheless we persisted in disputing these matters until we arranged that the Castilians should pay us the two instalments which were due under the Asiento, only yielding them the portion not yet due, which we could in no way collect and that they

---

[1] With Spain by the Treaty of 6th February 1715.

[2] The Treaty of 16th May 1703.

[3] By the Treaty of 18th June 1701 Spain was to pay 300,000 cruzados to the Portuguese Royal Guinea Company which supplied negro slaves for America, but see articles 15 and 16 of the Treaty of 6th February 1715.

[4] Captured by the Portuguese in the Algarve and at Rio de Janeiro.

should restore us the Colony of Sacramento, not as we held it before the war, but along with its district and permission to fortify it. Above all we obtained that all prizes made on both sides should be held good, in which the ships of Buenos Ayres were included and that no mention should be made of the restitution of the Houses[1] which the Castilians claimed; and without any orders we established for the first time an equality between His Majesty and the Catholic King, though in all previous treaties the contrary had been the rule. We have finished the work we set before us, but do not dare to say happily, because such a judgment can only be made by those who have the patience to read these *Memoirs*.

[1] The properties of Spanish nobles in Portugal.

III

INSTRUCTION OF 18TH JUNE 1709 TO THE
CONDE DE TAROUCA[1]

CONDE DE TAROUCA, Friend. It is very expedient for my service to send to the Congress of general peace which is about to be arranged a person of great authority and zeal as my Extraordinary Ambassador and first Plenipotentiary and as those qualities concur in you I was pleased to appoint you to this post, trusting from the great obligations you inherited that you will act with such care and discretion as may correspond to the confidence I manifest in you by charging you with this most important mission. As second Ambassador and Plenipotentiary to the said Congress I have also chosen Francisco de Sousa Pacheco[2] who has resided at the Hague for many years in the quality of my Extraordinary Envoy, so that he may help you in this negotiation with his experience and capacity. According to the last news from England and Holland, this is so far advanced that it is very important that on the receipt of the necessary dispatches with this Instruction you embark immediately on one of the packet-boats in this port to carry you to England; from there you will go to the Court of London to learn from my Extraordinary Envoy Dom Luis da Cunha the present state of the said negotiation and the orders that have been sent from that Court regarding it. And if you find that the Preliminaries which have been in discussion for some days are arranged

---

[1] This and the two following Instructions seem not to have been printed before. Though the Congress only opened in January 1712, Tarouca does not appear to have received any other formal Instructions, but when conditions changed in the interval, these were provided for and new orders sent to him and his colleagues by the Secretary of State. An example of this is furnished by the Questions of D. Luis da Cunha and the replies on a later page. The first two Instructions are translated from copies in cod. 4531 of the Biblioteca Nacional, Lisbon, fols. 7 and 13.

[2] He died in October 1709.

or nearly so, you will endeavour to pass over to Holland as soon as possible, so that before the Congress opens you may reach the Hague, where, as Francisco de Sousa notifies me, the Congress is to be held. And since it is proper that you should communicate to the Queen of Great Britain, my good sister and cousin, that you are going to the Peace Congress, you will ask a private audience and hand her the letter which I am writing to her with my own hand and you will accompany it with the expressions which you think most fitting to convince the Queen of my true friendship and ask her to interest herself in the success of your negotiations.

1. As soon as you arrive at the Hague you will try to learn from Francisco de Sousa Pacheco how the other Plenipotentiary Ambassadors of Crowned Heads are accustomed to act, so that you may do the same and you will hand to the States General the letter that will be given you in case the other Ambassadors and Plenipotentiaries to the Congress hand letters from their masters to the States, and you will endeavour to be received by them in the same form as the Plenipotentiaries of the Emperor, France, Castile and England.

2. I also order full powers to be supplied to you with eight signatures of mine in blank, so that you can use them when you think it necessary, because in view of the distance, the affairs you have in hand might be delayed through want of some order from me.

3. I have decided that you shall be given 20,000 cruzados as a grant in aid in the money current in this Kingdom and a conto as monthly allowance in the same form and as soon as the Congress opens, you will have a further 20,000 cruzados as grant in aid and a further conto as monthly allowance while it lasts and you are there by my orders, it being understood that, except in these cases, you will have no more than the 20,000 cruzados as grant in aid and the conto of monthly allowance.

4. You will endeavour to live on good terms with the Ministers of the Princes who are my Allies and especially with those of the Emperor Charles III, England and Holland, who will I hope help you in your aims and you will be able to obtain through them and through the Ministers of neutral Princes, the information and notices necessary for the success of your negotiations.

5. You must write by every post to the Secretary of State who will give you the cypher to be used for matters of secrecy and he will also hand you the cypher of the other Ministers I have in foreign Courts; you must also write to them and use their cyphers, when affairs demand this precaution.

6. I also order you to be supplied with all the Treaties which have been concluded between this Crown and those of Castile, England, France and the States General, together with the two of the Offensive and Defensive League and you will ask that these shall be promptly carried out.

7. As soon as I heard that peace was being considered, I ordered Francisco de Sousa Pacheco and D. Luis da Cunha to endeavour that England and Holland should arrange in the Preliminaries, not only for France to cede the rights she claimed in the territory bordering on Maranham as stipulated by Article 22 of the Offensive League, but all and every right and claim she may have to the Conquests of this Kingdom and because it is important to the above Powers that France shall have no pretext for taking possession of any of them and it is not right that now, when all the Allies are endeavouring to forward their own conveniences, they should fail to attend to mine, especially as they are interested in this one and if Francisco de Sousa has not obtained the above, you must at once ask them to oblige France to make that renunciation.

8. From the Treaties and secret Articles referred to, you will see which were the Castilian fortresses promised to be ceded to me as soon as King Charles III became master of the whole Monarchy and you must endeavour that at the same time as the Duke of Anjou has to leave that Kingdom and even earlier if you can arrange it, the promised fortresses which I judged necessary to the security of this realm are handed over to me; and it would not be just that, while those which the Emperor, the States General and the Duke of Savoy think necessary for their barrier, as they call it, are handed over to them, there should be delay in the transfer of those which I stipulated for mine, considering that I should not have entered into the League without this promise; and you must also ask that I may at the same time obtain restitution of the fortresses, cities, towns or places which the Castilians shall have occupied in this Kingdom and within a short space of

those that they have taken in its Conquests and especially the new Colony of Sacramento which was occupied in this war.

D. Luis da Cunha sent word that the Minister of Charles III at the Hague had asked the States General to induce me to accept an equivalent instead of the fortress of Badajoz and that the Ministers had replied that their only concern was to have the promised fortresses handed over to me; and if a similar proposal is made to you, you must declare that I will not admit any equivalent for Badajoz, nor for the other fortresses and you will inform the Ministers of England and Holland so that they may have what was promised me carried out, considering that both of them guaranteed the execution of the Treaty and you will only abstain from signing that of General Peace if it is sought to alter the League Treaty by denying me some of the promised fortresses.

9. If the Ministers of Charles III seek to excuse themselves from restoring the promised fortresses on the pretext that we did not carry on the war with the vigour and number of troops stipulated, you will reply that the war was made in such form that after the capture of the greater part of the Castilian fortresses on this frontier the army penetrated as far as Xadraque after occupying Madrid and had to retreat to Valencia through the events that happened and that I found myself obliged to sustain the army in that Kingdom and, after the loss of the battle of Almanza, in Aragon and Catalonia and to form another army in this Realm for its defence because England sent only six regiments here and Holland none: for this reason proper efforts were lacking on this side, notwithstanding the representations I had made in London and the Hague which were notified to the Catholic King by the Conde de Assumar and that it is notorious that I pledged all my royal revenues to maintain the two armies.

10. If the same Ministers demand the restitution of the Buenos Ayres ships seized in the Algarve and at Rio de Janeiro, desiring to compensate by their value for the fortresses they promised me, you will show them the reasons I had for that reprisal; you will find them in the memorandum of theologians and lawyers when I resolved on their seizure which will be handed to you and you will not allow the Catholic King to be compensated by the value of the said ships for what he is obliged by section 23 of the

Offensive League to pay to the Company of Guinea and the Indies, but rather you must ask that the money be paid in the form agreed and the documents he gave to the Company will be supplied to you.

11. You must endeavour that the Catholic King shall ratify the treaties which were celebrated between this Crown and that of Castile in the time of Charles II and all the preceding ones and if you can arrange that the importation of wheat, barley, horses and mules which is forbidden be allowed, it will be useful to obtain this without reciprocity if it can be done.

12. If the Preliminaries are not agreed and the whole Monarchy of Spain is not restored to Charles III, as is desired and if it must be divided between him and the Duke of Anjou, in this case you will ask that the former may keep Castile, the Indies and the Low Countries and that if any dominions are given to the latter, they may be in Italy and if it is designed to cede the province of Guipuscoa to France as was settled in the Partition Treaty made in the lifetime of Charles II, you will oppose this cession, because if France has that province it will be easy for her to take possession of Castile.

13. If the English or Dutch seek to have Gibraltar, Port Mahon, or some other port of Castile handed over to them as security for what King Charles owes them, you will try to hinder it as much as you can and request that they should at once withdraw the garrisons they have in those fortresses, because otherwise this Kingdom and that of Castile will be exposed to and the trade of all Europe dependent on the will of those nations; and you will do so in such a way as not to offend them. If it is desired to make the trade of the Indies free to all nations, you will endeavour that it may remain as it was in the time of Charles II and if it is thrown open, you must demand that this country shall enjoy the same liberty.

14. D. Luis da Cunha sends word that the Duke of Anjou does not wish to join in the peace and that he asks the King of France his grandfather to let him stay in Castile, even though he may not help him, because he has resolved not to leave that realm as long as he has Castilians who are willing to follow his fortunes; and therefore it is well that the most Christian King should undertake to remove his grandson from Castile since he put him

there and that this affair should not remain in such a state that the war will have to be continued in this Kingdom with English and Dutch aid to turn him out of Castile, for you are well aware that the Realm is not in a condition to continue that conquest, but if it has to be carried on, you must try to have it waged on the side of Catalonia, Andalusia and Galicia with the English and Dutch fleets so that the full weight of it may not fall on this Kingdom, remembering that while the Duke of Anjou remains in Castile there ought to be no armistice, but rather that the war should continue in every theatre in which it is waged at present.

15. If the Dutch, on the pretext of their barrier, claim to have some fortresses in the Low Countries ceded to them, or if England makes the same claim, you must endeavour that Flanders shall remain as it was in the time of Charles II and join the Ministers who oppose that cession, but you will do this in such a manner as not to give them cause for complaint.

16. As regards the Emperor and the Duke of Savoy, who desire France to cede them the fortresses which they think necessary for their security, you must help them in this aim and do the same in those of the other Allies so that they may also help you in mine, and if the same Allies shall also require that just as the Infantas of France who marry in Castile are excluded from the succession to that Kingdom, so those of Castile who marry in France shall be excluded from the succession to that Monarchy, you will support them because by this means the disturbance Europe suffers by the present war will be avoided for the future.

17. I have no doubt that France will seek to have the Electors of Bavaria and Cologne restored and in this particular, as also in that of the restoration of the Duchy of Mantua, you will join the Emperor's Ministers and you will do the same as regards the extinction or the contrary of the new Electorate instituted in the House of Brunswick.

18. The Elector Palatine has various claims on France, especially regarding the inheritance of the Duchess of Orleans and you must help his Ministers in them.

19. According to the present state of affairs and the declaration of the most Christian King in regard to the Prince of Wales, it is very probable that his interests will not be spoken of at the Congress, but if they are, or

if some allowance for him is mentioned, you must show yourself unconcerned in this particular so as not to give a cause of jealousy to England.

20. When the States General ratified the treaty of Defensive League, they omitted to ratify the second of the secret and separate articles for the reason you will find stated in the ratification itself. I charge you very particularly to ask them to ratify it and if you cannot obtain this, at least you will get them to continue with their tolerance.

21. I order you to be handed the accounts of what the States General owe, both for the stipulated subsidies as well as for bread, straw and barley supplied to their troops in this Kingdom and in that of Castile and you will ask them to pay you in the shortest possible periods; and as Francisco de Sousa Pacheco sends word that they seek to excuse themselves from this payment on the pretext that I had not the number of men to which I was bound, you will reply to them that up to the battle of Almanza I had in the army and in this Realm more than I was obliged and that if I had less infantry after the loss of that battle on account of the many regiments which were lost, this deficiency was made up for by my having to maintain an army in this Realm for its defence and by the men I have in Catalonia. This cost me double expense, chiefly because the corps that remained there was of 4000 horse or thereabouts, for the eight regiments I maintained there came to as much and five of infantry and in this Realm fourteen of cavalry and thirty-four of infantry, and it is notorious that it costs much more to maintain regiments of cavalry than of infantry; to this must be added the losses I suffered in that battle and in this year's fight, since on both occasions the artillery and baggage on which I had spent a considerable sum were lost and you will refute their pretexts with these reasons and others that occur to you.

22. If the said States shall excuse themselves from promptly paying this debt on the ground of their small means at the present, you may take in payment the three million florins, beyond the cost of fortifications, for the security of which the fortresses of Cochin and Cananor[1] were pledged, and when their debt exceeds mine you will endeavour that Cochin shall

[1] These two fortresses were captured from the Portuguese by the forces of the Dutch East India Company in 1662-3.

be immediately handed over to me and on your informing me of how much remains for the restitution of Cananor, I will instruct you if it should or should not be redeemed.

23. If the States seek to write off this debt with the value of the Castilian ship which Vice-Admiral Wassenar drove on shore in the Algarve, you will satisfy them with the reply given to their Plenipotentiary here when he spoke of this matter, with which the States were content, and you will do the same about the claim for the goods which the subjects of that Republic said they had on board the Buenos Ayres ships which were seized at Rio de Janeiro and copies of both replies will be delivered to you.

24. You must also ask them to pay us for the powder they have not handed over and for the arms which they were bound to supply and the account of the debt will be handed to you and if you can arrange for both of these things to be paid you in cash, it will be very convenient, since this Realm has no lack of powder and arms.

25. If the Dutch wish to make some arrangement about the sale of the Setubal salt and agree to take a certain quantity, you will send word and forward the terms of the project, so that after hearing the persons who produce salt in that town, I may decide what I consider best and you will act in the same way if like proposals are made to you by Swedes, Danes and men of Hamburg.

26. The English have so far continued to pay the monthly sums to which they were obliged by the Treaty, but you must ask that they shall pay all the cost of the troops in Catalonia from the time when the Queen of Great Britain decided that they should be paid on her account and that this payment shall continue until the troops are restored to this Realm, doing your best to secure their return by land if King Charles III comes with his army to Madrid, or if he desires to take my troops and his to that Court; but if the army is to separate in Catalonia, you will ask for the infantry to come by sea and the cavalry by land as commodiously as possible and until they reach this Realm, all the expense must be on account of the said Queen, as has been stated.

27. You will be handed an account of the powder and arms owing by England so that you may ask for payment of what is found to be due.

⟨ 26 ⟩

28. I have already ordered you to endeavour that France shall give up the rights she claimed in the territory adjoining Maranham as also any claim she may have in my Conquests and although this Crown and that did not declare war, yet as peace was interrupted by the hostilities which were carried on by one side and another, it will be advisable for a new treaty to be made between the two for re-establishing friendship and as regards commerce containing the conditions of the Treaty of 1667; and it is very necessary to have a declaration in it that the French of Cayenne, or any other subjects of France, shall not trade in Maranham or in any other of my Conquests and if the occasion is favourable, you will endeavour to improve the Treaty of Commerce between the two Crowns, even in Europe and I have no doubt that the English and Dutch will help you because of the useful results they may expect.

29. Should the King of France seek to have the goods of the Buenos Ayres ships seized in the Algarve and at Rio de Janeiro restored to his subjects, you will give him the same reply as to the States General.

30. If the King of Sweden seeks to have the treaty made between this Crown and that renewed and ratified, you will make no objection to the new ratification and if he makes proposals for a new treaty, you will send word and forward the project and you will act in the same way with the Kings of Denmark and Prussia and also if our Allies, after peace has been concluded, want to make a new league between themselves for the security of the peace and of Charles III.

31. If the King of Sweden and the other neutral Princes aspire to be mediators in this Peace, you will not interest yourself in the claims of this or that, but follow the opinion of the Allies.

32. Usually at the opening of a Congress it is arranged for passports to be sent at once for the free passage of posts and you will ask France and Castile to allow them, so that you can send me expresses when you have any matter that requires it.

33. To avoid preferences between Crowned Heads in seats and signatures, it was established in the last Congress of Ryswick that the Plenipotentiaries should take their seats as they entered and that each should sign his project and treaty; in this Congress it is very likely that the same course will be

followed to avoid disputes, but, if not, you will send word and abstain from going to the Congress if you do not find a way of going without being preceded by anyone; in the meantime Francisco de Sousa Pacheco will be able to go in his quality of Envoy Plenipotentiary but he will not take that of Ambassador, as I am sending to inform him, because as long as he is Envoy and the others are Ambassadors he cannot have any disputes, but if the other Plenipotentiaries do not possess the rank of Ambassadors, then he must only allow himself to be preceded by those of the Emperor, France and Castile and if England and the other Crowns try to precede him, he will not go and you and he will endeavour to negotiate in private conferences until you receive orders from me.

34. If the Kings of Poland Augustus and Stanislaus send Ambassadors to the Congress, you will recognise the one whom our Allies recognise, or both if recognised by them.

35. You will send me word of all that occurs which is not provided for in this Instruction and if the matter does not allow this delay, I trust the solution of it to your prudence. Gaspar de Oliveira wrote it in Lisbon the 18th June 1709, I Diogo de Mendonça Corte Real subscribed it. King.

Instruction for the Conde de Tarouca whom your Majesty now sends as his Extraordinary Ambassador and first Plenipotentiary to the Congress of General Peace. For your Majesty to see.

IV
INSTRUCTION OF 30TH JUNE 1709 TO THE
CONDE DE TAROUCA

CONDE DE TAROUCA, Friend. After the preparation of the Instruction which will be handed to you with this, the English packet-boat arrived and my Extraordinary Envoy in London D. Luis da Cunha sent by it the 40 Articles of Preliminaries of the General Peace which were signed at the Hague on the 28th of last month and I have ordered them to be given to you; it was stipulated by them that the whole Spanish Monarchy should be restored to Charles III, except such part as was to be given to me and to the Duke of Savoy and therefore I again order you to endeavour to have the fortresses which were promised me restored as soon as possible, as I have already charged you. The Most Christian King also promises in the same Preliminaries to consent that I shall enjoy all the advantages established in my favour in the Treaties of Alliance and this seems to refer to the renunciation which the Allies promised that the same King would make of the right he claimed to have in the territories adjoining Maranham, and you will endeavour to get him to carry this out at once and also the renunciation of any rights he claims to have in my Conquests.

An Armistice of two months was agreed upon in the same Preliminaries, but it cannot be of any use to me or to King Charles III because the Duke of Anjou was not a party to the settlement of the said Preliminaries, moreover by means of them France obtained a suspension of hostilities in these parts where the League had larger forces, while the war is to continue in this Kingdom and in Catalonia where the Duke of Anjou is in the ascendant and it is not likely that he will agree to leave Castile, seeing that he is strong enough to defend himself; therefore as soon as you arrive, you must represent to the Congress that if the suspension of hostilities cannot be general for the reason mentioned, all the Allies shall continue the war in every part in which it is now being waged, because this is the only way to compel France to remove the Duke of Anjou from Spain and it is not fitting that after the two months' armistice is over, the proper measures should be considered for making the Duke of Anjou leave Spain, because, in the meanwhile, he will add to his forces, since France, being relieved from the war, even though she may not furnish him with men as she promises, will be able to help him with the means of raising them, and lastly you must declare that as the principal object of this war was to get the same Duke out of Spain and place Charles III on the throne of that Monarchy, as long as these two things are not secured, there ought not to be a suspension of hostilities anywhere and you will add the other reasons that occur to you in this matter.

To avoid embarrassments and difficulties about the ceremonial, it was arranged in the last article of the said Preliminaries that none of the Plenipotentiaries should declare himself as an Ambassador until the day of the signature of the Treaties and you must observe this and since this quality is not necessary for the course of the negotiation, it was my pleasure that Francisco de Sousa Pacheco should take part in it and in its conclusion as Plenipotentiary, in the quality of Envoy Extraordinary which he holds.

In the other Instruction you are informed that the States General ratified the Treaty of the Defensive League and one of the separate articles, but reserved the ratification of the second article and though their Plenipotentiary has the ratifications here, these have not been exchanged until now, because he has to hand over with them the discharge of the States declaring that they have received the 850,000 cruzados which the said Plenipotentiary received from the Treasurer of salt at Setubal, by which amount the States admitted they had been paid, not only for what I was obliged to hand them for the Setubal salt and their rights under the Treaty of 1669 but also for the artillery I was bound to restore to them by the Treaty of 1661,[1] and his reason for not handing over this discharge was that he entrusted the special power he had from his masters to give it to Roque Monteiro Paim who negotiated with him and this was not to be found after his death, therefore I order you to hand over the ratification

---

[1] These two Treaties are printed in Borges de Castro, *op. cit.* vol. I.

of the Treaty of the Defensive League and of the separate article and you will exchange them for those of the States, if they order you to be given the discharge for the said 850,000 cruzados which their Plenipotentiary received, in case they have not sent it to their Plenipotentiary. Lisbon. 30th June 1709. I Diogo de Mendonça Corte Real subscribed it. King.

Second instruction which your Majesty ordered to be prepared for the Conde de Tarouca after his having been acquainted with the Preliminary Articles for the General Peace as therein declared. For your Majesty to see.

V
INSTRUCTION OF 6TH AUGUST 1709 TO THE
CONDE DE TAROUCA[1]

CONDE DE TAROUCA, Friend. In view of the frustration of the peace negotiations, the preliminaries of which had been arranged at the Court of the Hague, owing to the fact that the King of France would not sign them, I was pleased to order you to suspend your journey to Holland whither I was sending you in the quality of my Extraordinary Ambassador and first Plenipotentiary to the Peace Congress, but as it is proper that my Allies should help me with the needful succour and subsidies to continue the war, it is my pleasure that you go immediately to the Court of London in a private capacity, as I determined two years ago, to represent on my part to the Queen that it is absolutely necessary, if the war is to be carried on here with vigour, that the succours I asked for last year should be sent to this Realm; these were twenty regiments of infantry, including those that are here, one thousand five hundred horse and a fleet or squadron able to make a diversion on the side of Andalusia. These are the succours which her Ambassador the Earl of Galway stated to be necessary for carrying on an offensive war against Castile, considering also that this could not be done without first occupying Badajoz for whose siege the aids referred to were required. And as this representation was made last year by D. Luis da Cunha, my Extraordinary Envoy in London, he will inform you of the present position and the persons with whom you must negotiate this matter and of their inclinations, so that you may do your business better; and as soon as you reach that Court, you will ask for a private audience of the Queen and hand her my autograph letter, which you will receive with this instruction and after expressing to her my

[1] Dr. Eduardo Brazão kindly copied the Portuguese text of this document which is in the Tarouca Archives.

sincere friendship and love for her person and my desire, not only to continue our close alliance but to execute every part of it, you will show her that this cannot be done without those succours and you will state all the reasons which I trust to your prudence and experience arising from the present condition of the Realm and you will ask her to send me the officers stipulated by the Treaty and a train of artillery also.

As you have no diplomatic character, you must not claim the privileges of an Ambassador or public Minister, or even that of the title of this Realm, because the English lords do not have it there, and thus you are only entitled to the immunity due by the law of nations to all persons who go on any negotiation with a Letter of Credence.

I order the said D. Luis da Cunha to understand that he must give you the best place in his house and coach and in any other part also, and you will do the same with him in your house and coach, but you must remember not to precede him in the Conferences and thus if it is necessary for any to be held, you will go alone to them and when it is advisable for him to go, you will stay away and by this means avoid his preceding you in the said Conferences, because as he has the diplomatic quality and you have not, if both were together, he ought to precede you and when he has to go and confer, he will first arrange with you what he shall say and you will do the same when you have to go.

When you talk with the ministers of that Court about the succours, you will try to persuade them that as Castile is the head of the Monarchy, that realm ought to be conquered, seeing that the Castilians resist as we know by experience; for there is no doubt that the other states of the said Monarchy will follow the fortunes of the principal part and that this conquest cannot be made without the said succours which the King Charles III needs, chiefly because the Castilians have resolved to defend themselves, even if the King of France abandons them, as he promised in the Preliminaries which he did not sign, and for this purpose they are raising twenty-two regiments of infantry and increasing their cavalry by a further ten horsemen in each company: for the slight efforts hitherto made for the Spanish war led the Castilians, who were encouraged by the victories of Almanza and Godinha, to take this resolution which may be very prejudicial to the common cause, if proper reinforcements are not sent at once to this Realm and to Catalonia, because it will be both impossible to carry on an offensive war such as is needed, but even to keep this Realm and that Principality secure; and if this happens, the efforts made against France will do little to compel the Duke of Anjou to leave Spain, which was the principal object of the League, for France will never oblige the Castilians to drive the said Duke out of Castile whilst they have forces to defend themselves, nor will he abandon the Realm as long as he thinks he can keep it.

In view of this it seems absolutely necessary, if this war is to be ended, to wage it against the Castilians with the greatest possible vigour and as I have so often been promised that I should receive succours and these have not arrived (for even those destined for me were sent to Flanders), you will not be satisfied with promises but endeavour to get them carried into effect and the men sent in time to be able to serve in the spring campaign; if they are to do this, they must leave England in January and if it be possible for regiments to bring baggage wagons, you will ask for them, because they are very lacking in this Realm.

I charged D. Luis da Cunha to ask that the Queen should pay all the troops I have in Catalonia, because hitherto she has only sent 80,000 pounds sterling for their subsistence and this is not enough, as is shown by the account sent to D. Luis and you will learn the state of this matter from him and endeavour to get the Queen to bear all that expense, if he has not succeeded in doing so and declare that if she does not, I shall have to recall the said troops through inability to maintain them in that Principality, and you will also say that as I have ordered the pay of the officers and soldiers to be augmented, it is just that my subsidies should also be increased, as I have instructed the said D. Luis to represent.

The same envoy will inform you of the state of my claim to be paid what remained owing to the Queen of Great Britain, my Aunt,[1] who is in glory, in respect of the revenues which were assigned to her for her maintenance and you will give your assistance in this matter in such wise as seems proper to you and do the same in all the rest.

[1] Queen Catharine, wife of Charles II.

I leave to your prudence and zeal the matters not provided for in this Instruction which you cannot first send an account of and wait for my decision, for I am confident that you will act in all of them according to my interests.

I was pleased to order you to be given fourteen thousand cruzados in the money current in this kingdom as a grant in aid and they will be deducted from the twenty thousand which I resolved you should have as grant in aid on your going as my Extraordinary Ambassador to the Peace Congress; when you go there in the said quality and during the time that you are without it I ordered that you should be given one thousand cruzados as a monthly allowance free from the risks of exchange and you will make use for this expense of the thirty thousand cruzados you had to go to Holland and I am informing the Junta of the monthly allowance and grant in aid which I bestow on you, so that when the thirty thousand cruzados are exhausted, it may continue to pay you the monthly allowances.

Together with the Instruction for the Peace negotiations you were handed the cypher for your correspondence and those which belonged to the other Ministers and you will use them in the matters demanding that caution. Although your principal charge is as above, you will have understood that you must give particular attention to finding out the methods used in the peace, so as to give me an account of all you discover, and even if the succours are granted to you and sent to this Kingdom, you must remain in London till further orders, unless you learn for certain that the peace conferences are being renewed and that the Plenipotentiaries of the other Princes are going to take part in them, because then you must at once go to where they are held and take with you all the papers which I ordered to be handed to you for this business and in this case, even though your claims have not been met, you must depart and leave them in the hands of D. Luis da Cunha so that he may continue to press them. Written in Lisbon the sixth of August 1709. I Diogo de Mendonça Corte Real subscribed it. King. Instruction to be used by the Conde de Tarouca in the negotiation for which your Majesty now sends him to the Court of England. For your Majesty to see.

VI

QUESTIONS OF D. LUIS DA CUNHA WITH HIS MAJESTY'S DECISION IN THE MARGIN[1]

THE KING

I

They must insist on the Duke leaving Spain, but if England and Holland, notwithstanding the opposition of the other Allies, make a treaty by which the said Prince stays in Spain, they will do the same, provided that at least the barrier promised in the League treaty is secured for this Kingdom and if only England signs, while Holland joins the Princes who oppose it, they will raise doubts about signing and send word.

I

As the interests of Portugal clearly require that the Duke of Anjou should leave Spain, since she entered the Alliance and made war on him for that purpose and as it is no less probable that he will be left there, it is necessary to know whether the Ministers of the King, our Lord, ought to raise doubts or support those invented by others, or such as naturally arise, so that the Congress may be delayed, or broken up.

2

They should not hinder the choice of a mediator or mediators and may consent to England holding that position and the others proposed by the rest of the Allies.

2

If any of the Plenipotentiaries, either to gain time or because they think it is to their interest, suggest that an impartial mediator is needed to keep the minutes for the purpose of registering memoranda, requisitions and protests, so as to avoid the disorder which would ensue if everything was read in full Congress, the said Ministers ought to know whether to concur in this, even though the English maintain the contrary.

[1] This document was printed for the first time by Dr. Eduardo Brazão in *Portugal no Congresso de Utrecht*. It comes from the Tarouca Archives.

3

This has been answered in the preceding.

3

If the Plenipotentiaries of the Queen insinuate that they are ready to undertake this work and meet with opposition because the full power to treat as an interested party does not go with the credential of impartial mediator, it will be equally useful to know whether English mediation should be accepted, or whether those that wish another should be supported, because although it is said that France and Spain would be chiefly prejudiced by the mediation of their own side, yet as we all maintain that she is in accord with those two Powers and wishes to end the war at once, she is more suspect than allied.

4

They must negotiate with the Ministers of France and Castile by means of England, if the affair is put in the terms considered in the answer to the first question.

4

Supposing there to be no difficulty in this matter about the English Ministers acting as mediators by tacit consent and privately hearing the Ministers of France and Spain, it is necessary to know if those of His Majesty may treat with them directly.

5

If most of the Allied Ministers oppose Venetian mediation, which France and Spain will probably not admit, according to present conditions, they will vote for exclusion, so that it will not take place if the majority accept it.

5

As the Republic of Venice desires this mediation and it is possible that Holland will help her through distrust of England, it is right that His Majesty should say beforehand if he has any objections to the said Republic, remembering that the Emperor will offer many and not without reason.

6

In the case stated in the resolutions on the first and fourth questions, they

6

If England and Holland straightway admit the Ambassadors of the Duke

may treat with the Ministers of Castile and France, previously paying due attention to those of the Emperor and showing them that this Kingdom cannot continue the war without England and Holland for the reasons that are well known.

7

If this case occurs, they should do the same as they suppose the Ministers of England and Holland will do.

of Anjou in the quality of King of Castile, since they have already recognised him once as such, it is also well to know if the Ambassador of His Majesty who took the same step should follow them, or preserve some measure with the Emperor.

7

As England pretends not to have decided anything as regards continental Spain, although there is no doubt that she has agreed to the Duke of Anjou staying there, the English Ministers, to save appearances with the world, this nation, the Emperor, ourselves and the Duke of Savoy, may insist with the French Minister, although by arrangement with him, on the plan for restitution of the said monarchy in such wise as to make a merit with that Prince of these feigned efforts and he will be offended at the others, because they are sincere and in this case it is necessary to know the line that should be taken.

8

They must insist on the fortresses which have been asked for, besides those promised and be content with the latter, if they cannot get more, declaring however that the fortresses must be handed over before the ratification and they will accept no equivalent, but if this is insisted upon after it has been rejected, they will send word and ask time for the reply.

8

As England has arranged its affairs and those of Holland are on the way to be settled, so far as I can gather it is clear that the Congress will not last long for the reasons mentioned, wherefore it is necessary that if our new claim to the fortresses of Ciudad Rodrigo, Alcanizas and Zamora to cover the Provinces of Beira and Tras-os-Montes is just, we should know how far we ought to insist in case of opposition, or if they should be accepted if offered instead of Vigo, Tuy, etc.: as it seems that we are covered on that side and we ask the said fortresses for our security.

9

This is answered in the preceding.

9

If the English Ministers begin to show that they will not only not support the new claim, but also grow cool about getting us the advantages stipulated by the Treaty, we must be instructed as to how far we ought to insist and what in this case we should support with most vigour, after seeing that it is useless to hope to obtain all of them.

10

The orders were that as the Preliminaries contain a declaration about the barrier for England and Holland, that solemnly promised to Portugal should also be mentioned and this is now out of the question if the Preliminaries are not amended.

10

Your Majesty ordered me in the last resort to get the Kingdom of Portugal separately mentioned in the Preliminaries with regard to freedom of trade, in the same way as England and Holland. This article of the Preliminaries deals with the trade of France and it is the one which the two Powers settled upon before entering the Congress and so it would be well for us to represent the points in which ours is damaged and what ought to be asked to improve it, for we really do not know, at least I do not and I am only sure that as regards England it cannot be more disadvantageous and with little hope of giving it any balance.

11

They must make the same claim for liberty of trade in the Indies, but not for establishments there.

11

Regarding the trade of the Spanish Indies, as it is said that the enemies give England various establishments in those parts for her security, I know not if your Majesty's order extends so far as that we should make the same claim.

12

Using the caution referred to so as not to offend the English, they will try to prevent the latter from establishing themselves in the South Sea because of the injury they will be able to cause to the trade of Buenos Ayres and Rio de Janeiro.

As I do not hear that the Dutch are to get the same advantage, no doubt they will try to hinder that of England in an underhand manner, so that if it is thought to be harmful to us also, we should have orders to join with the Dutch, although with the same caution.

13

They will try to hinder it with the same caution, if they think there is a hope of success, even though the Duke of Anjou stays in Spain.

I recall having seen in the Instructions of the Conde de Tarouca that it was thought inadvisable that the English should remain in Port Mahon, but as events have changed so much, it would be well to know if our interests are no longer the same in this particular also, because if the Duke of Anjou stays in Spain, it may be thought that it would suit us for the English to have one foot in Gibraltar and one in Port Mahon, so that the French may not be entirely masters of the Mediterranean and that the Castilians may have this kind of bit, although it will not be for long, as we saw in the case of Tangier.

14

This needs no reply because it is an observation and not a question.

I do not ask anything regarding the other matters treated of in this Peace, because I have no doubt that we shall be compelled to be unconcerned witnesses only to report them.

15

They will follow what the other Allies do and each of the Plenipotentiaries may write privately, when he thinks proper.

Although the Courts are not accustomed to send more than one dispatch to their Ministers and these do not write separately, it will nevertheless be well for his Majesty to order what is his pleasure.

16

When this happens, they will hear all that is proposed to them and then reply that as it is a matter outside their commission, they cannot answer without sending word.

If the Ministers of England quarrel with those of France, so that a rupture of negotiations is to be feared and these propose to those of the King our Lord that his most Christian Majesty and the Duke of Anjou will give us the same advantages if we leave the Alliance, it is well for us to know if we should listen, refuse or keep them in doubt.

17

This is answered in the preceding.

Supposing that these Ministers of England do not disagree with those of France, as hitherto, because the latter must wish to make certain of the Peace and the former will not be in a state to threaten them with the war and union of the Alliance, yet if the French offer us a separate Treaty with some real advantages, we must be instructed what to do.

18

They must send word, because the Defensive League is made with England and Holland against France and Castile.

If during the Congress the Ministers of France suggest to those of his Majesty a private Alliance after the conclusion of the general Peace, it would also be well to know if they should be encouraged in this idea.

This is answered in the first.

If it happens, though I do not expect it, that the Allies, ill-satisfied with the conditions of the Peace (and we have the same reason), will not sign it and only England signs, what side should we follow?

On these questions of D. Luis da Cunha His Majesty was pleased to determine what is contained in the replies in their margin and he orders you[1] to observe it, unless unexpected events occur to alter what the said Lord resolved, because in this case you must send word, if you can and if you cannot, His Majesty leaves it to your prudence and I am advising D. Luis da Cunha in the same sense. May Our Lord preserve you for many years. Lisbon. 29th January 1712.

Diogo de Mendonça Corte Real.

---

[1] These lines were evidently addressed to the Conde de Tarouca, though Dr. Brazão does not say so.

NOTE

When the proofs of this work had already been corrected a new book by Dr. Eduardo Brazão appeared: *Relações externas de Portugal, Reinado de D. João V.* It contains the three Instructions (see p. 19 *supra*) and a quantity of important diplomatic correspondence of the Conde de Tarouca and others which had not been printed before or even known.